CIVIL DISOBEDIENCE AND THE NEW COVENANT

Dr. Carroll Parish

Unless otherwise identified, all Scripture quotations in this publication are taken from the *Holy Bible, New Kings James Version, copyright 1982 by Thomas Nelson, Inc.*

Scriptures marked NIV are from the Holy Bible, New International Version®, NIV® Copyright ©1973, 1978, 1984, 2011 by Biblica, Inc.® Used by permission. All rights reserved worldwide.

Scriptures marked AMP are taken from the Amplified Bible (AMP). Copyright © 2015 by The Lockman Foundation, La Habra, CA 90631. All rights reserved.

Dreamy (5x8) Self-Publishing Template © 2017 Renee Fisher https://www.reneefisher.com

Special Thanks to my wife, Debbie, for proof reading. Special Thanks to Renee Fisher & Co. for editing and placing on Amazon. Special Thanks to Marcy Davis for designing the cover.

Table of Contents

Major Text

"Let every soul be subject to the governing authorities. For there is no authority except from God, and the authorities that exist are appointed by God. Therefore whoever resists the authority resists the ordinance of God, and those who resist will bring judgment on themselves. For rulers are not a terror to good works, but to evil. Do you want to be unafraid of the authority? Do what is good, and you will have praise from the same. For he is God's minister to you for good. But if you do evil, be afraid; for he does not bear the sword in vain; for he is God's minister, an avenger to *execute* wrath on him who practices evil. Therefore *you* must be subject, not only because of wrath but also for conscience' sake. For because of this you also pay taxes, for they are God's ministers attending continually to this very thing. Render therefore to all their due: taxes to whom taxes *are due,* customs to whom customs, fear to whom fear, honor to whom honor" (Romans 13:1-8).

Foreword

We live in a world that is greatly divided. We have conservatives and liberals; rich and poor, highly educated and others not so much. Some have been raised in good solid Christian homes while others may have had no parental nor Christian upbringing at all.

All of us react to life through the lens of these things. But that does not mean that we have to stay in these places or conditions. Because of what Jesus did on the Cross we have full redemption provided for us. We can read the Bible and find answers to all of life. Those answers will be found, specifically in the New Testament (Covenant), through aligning ourselves to Jesus and His plan for our individual lives and what He is doing today on the earth, and what His plan is for the future.

As we look at the subject of "Civil Disobedience" we might realize a conflict in our thinking about it. We could possibly see a conflict between obeying authority and individual liberties, and these certainly do exist. But which is most important? Which one is more Biblical? Where does governmental authority fit in to this equation?

These are some of the topics we will cover.

While this is far from exhaustive, my hope is that it will be useful to cause us to examine it so that we might be better prepared for the future and our place in it.

Chapter One:
Forerunners

Henry David Thoreau (1817-1862) was a transcendentalist, which was a society that officially only existed for ten years but was extremely influential both in his day and today. This belief system was a mixture of eastern religions, humanism, with a little Bible thrown in for good measure.

Thoreau's attitude toward reform involved his transcendental efforts to live a spiritually meaningful life in nature. As a transcendentalist, Thoreau believed that reality existed only in the spiritual world, and the solution to people's problems was the free development of emotions ("Transcendentalism").

Transcendentalism was a philosophy that promoted self-reliance, intuition, and independence, and was heavily influenced by the European Romantic movement as well as Eastern religious texts. The three basic ideas (Experience, Self-reliance, and Worship) in Thoreau's Walden deals specifically with one theme: "Simplicity". To Thoreau, simplicity in experience, simplicity in self-reliance, and simplicity in worship breeds the finer things in life.

When God or the Bible is referred to in his writings, they are mentioned only to placate his religious readers but without any indication of a personal experience with the God of heaven.

In his book, *Civil Disobedience*, Thoreau indicates his belief that one should oppose all governmental or spiritual authority if it seeks to hinder the three tenets of transcendentalism. Some of his beliefs still run rampant through European and American ideology.

Dietrich Bonhoeffer (1906-1945) was an author, pastor, philosopher and a great hero of the faith to many people. The thing that most of us know about him is his stance to defeat Hitler and the German war machine that attempted to conquer Europe and the world. This cost him his life which he was willing to give for the freedom of others.

Perhaps his most notable statement is, "When God calls a man, he bids him come and die." Below I have given some statements from him to show his commitment to Jesus' Lordship and his willingness to follow Christ even to death.

"If Christian teaching does not guide us in the use of freedom and God is denied, all obligations and responsibilities that are sacred and binding on man are undermined."[1]

"In the earlier stages of his career Bonhoeffer accepted the traditional Lutheran view that there was a sharp distinction between politics and religion. Gradually, however, he revised his opinion, not because he was a politician or because he refused to give Caesar his due, but because he came to recognize that the political authority in Germany had become entirely corrupt and immoral and

---

[1] *The Cost of Discipleship* page 23 copyright Simon & Schuster, New York 1959

that a false faith is capable of terrible and monstrous things. For Bonhoeffer Hitler was the Antichrist, the arch-destroyer of the world and its basic values, the Antichrist who enjoys destruction, slavery, death and extinction for their own sake, the Antichrist who wants to pose the negative as positive and as creative.

"Bonhoeffer was firmly and rightly convinced that it is not only a Christian right but a Christian duty towards God to oppose tyranny, that is, government which is no longer based on natural law and the law of God."[2]

I would highly recommend reading or re-reading The Cost of Discipleship. It will challenge us to a higher level of commitment to Jesus' Lordship.

Francis Schaeffer (1912-1984) was a Christian theologian, philosopher, and Presbyterian pastor. He was the author of twenty-two books among them is *A Christian Manifesto*, which I highly recommend.

With his wife, Edith, Francis founded L'Abri Fellowship, an international study center and community in Switzerland.

From the cover of *A Christian Manifesto*,[3] I quote the following: "It happened so subtly that few people noticed at first. Little by little, morality and freedom started to crumble. It came first in government, to education, in the media-and finally it began to shake our families and our own lives.

"Something fundamental has changed. Law and government no longer provide a foundation of justice and morality but have become the means of licensing moral perversions of all kinds. Education has become the enemy of religious truth and values. And the media have provided

---

[2] Cit. pages 29-30

[3] *A Christian Manifesto* copyright 1981 and published by Crossway Books, Westchester, Ill.

the means for propagating the change.

"In this book Dr. Schaeffer shows why this has happened. First, he shows how we have failed to understand the problem-to see that the whole foundation for society has shifted radically from its original Judeo-Christian basis to a humanistic basis. As the humanistic view takes over, it necessarily destroys the whole way of life built upon the Judeo-Christian heritage. Second, Dr. Schaeffer calls for a massive movement-in government, law and all of life-to reestablish the Judeo-Christian foundation and turn the tide of moral decadence and loss of freedom.

"This book is literally a call for Christians to change the course of history-by returning to biblical Truth and by allowing Christ to be Lord in all of life. To do this, Schaeffer says, will involve a head-on confrontation with the false view that material or energy, shaped by chance, is the final reality.

"Schaeffer's provocative conclusion is that when the state directly defies the absolute law of God, its authority becomes illegitimate. [4]In this case, the Christian is bound to resist the state by whatever means necessary-through direct legal and political action, and possibly through massive demonstrations of civil disobedience."

I will give a few more quotes from Schaeffer's book that may shed some light on the idea of Civil Disobedience.

"True spirituality covers all of reality. There are things the Bible tells us as absolutes which are sinful-which do not conform to the character of God. But aside from these the Lordship of Christ covers all of life and all of life

---

[4] What should our actions be when this occurs? Psalm 75:7 says, "But God is the Judge, He puts down one and exalts another." How can we participate with Him in this? Voting, prayer, and perhaps "Civil Disobedience."

equally. It is not only that true spirituality covers all of life, but it covers all parts of the spectrum of life equally. In this sense there is nothing concerning reality that is not spiritual.

"There are Christians who believe, let us say, the truth of creation, the truth of the virgin birth, the truth of Christ's miracles, Christ's substitutionary death, and His coming again. But they stop there with these and other individual truths. When I say that Christianity is true I mean it is true to total reality-the total to what is, beginning with the central reality, the objective existence of personal-infinite God. Christianity is not just a series of truths but Truth-Truth about all of reality. And the holding to that Truth intellectually-and then in some poor way living upon that Truth, the Truth of what is-bring forth not only certain personal results, but also governmental and legal results."[5]

Schaeffer gave some definitions that would be good for us to recognize. He said, "*Humanitarianism* is being kind and helpful to people, treating people humanly. The *humanities* are the study of literature, art, music, etc. – those things which are the products of human creativity. *Humanism* is the placing of Man at the center of all things and making him the measure of all things."[6]

"The Reformation got rid of the encrustations that had been added to the Judeo-Christian world view and clarified the point of authority-with authority resting in the Scripture rather than church and Scripture, or state and Scripture. This not only had meaning in regard to doctrine but clarified the base for law. That base was God's written law, back through the New Testament to Moses' written Law: and the content and authority of that written Law is rooted back to Him who is the final reality."[7]

---

[5] Cit. pages 19-20

[6] Cit. page 23

[7] Cit. page 28

"Thus, neither church nor state were equal to, let alone above, that Law. The base for law is not divided, and no one has the right to place anything, including king, state or church, above the content of God's law."[8]

I would strongly recommend that you read *The Christian Manifesto*. I believe it will strengthen and encourage each of us to take a strong stance on the authority of God and His Word.

---

[8] Cit. page 29

Chapter Two:
Preference or
Conviction

While we are dealing with the topic of "Civil Disobedience" we need to know if what we believe or our plan of action is coming from a preference or a conviction.

As a young attorney, David C. Gibbs Jr. could hardly believe his ears as the pastor relayed how his church was being sued by the state for operating its ministry. As he reviewed the legal documents, Dr. Gibbs was astonished that such a thing could happen in modern America. From that very first case through the present day, God has blessed Dr. Gibbs' commitment to legally help churches, pastors, and Christians free of charge. The ministry has grown substantially through God's blessing over the last 40 years as attorneys, legal assistants, and other ministry workers have joined the team of "legal missionaries."

Shared here are excerpts from his book, *Conviction vs. Preference*, by Attorney David C. Gibbs Jr., Christian Law Association, Conneaut, Ohio 44030. These are actual incidents that have occurred during court proceedings.

When a Christian stands to defend his beliefs in a court room, his testimony becomes quite critical, for the court has said a man cannot hold his beliefs if he cannot describe them. A belief is not a hunch. It is not a feeling or an "it seems to me."

There are people who have gone to the witness stand and after stating what they believe are asked, "Well, why do you believe that? Can you show me that in the word of God?" Some do not even know if what they believe is there, but reply with "it sort of seems to me." The problem the court has with a "well, it seems to me," is that feelings change rapidly and as a consequence, a hunch or a feeling, or an "it seems to me" will not be honored.

In a court of law, a defendant must be able to state his beliefs from the Bible orally. The court does not expect eloquence, but it does expect the defendant to be able to explain his or her beliefs in a simple and concise manner. It also requires knowledge of those beliefs. This becomes important because often we like to hide behind a title. We may claim to be a "separated fundamentalist" or "a Christian," which are descriptive terms that may have to be described more fully. In the matter of beliefs and believers, the court realized there must be a test to determine which beliefs are upheld and which beliefs will not be honored and protected by the First Amendment of the U.S. Constitution.

In 1972, the court came down with such a test. Ironically, that test case involved Christian education. An Amish man who lived in the state of Wisconsin by the name of Jonas Yoder told the state that he would no longer send his children to the state school. The state of Wisconsin advised him that he must, to which he replied, "I don't think you hear me. I am not going to send my children to your school." Mr. Yoder was threatened with being sued if he refused to comply but still, he refused. He was warned that if he was sued and if the state won the case, he could go to jail. His only response was that he would not send his children to the school. Even under the threat of losing his children, he refused to change his mind, explaining that his religious beliefs prohibited him from complying with the demand.

Mr. Yoder did not fare very well in court. He lost the case and was told that now that he had had his day in court, he must comply with the ruling. He still refused, never altering his position and he found out something very interesting. After losing his appeal, his case went to the U. S. Supreme Court, where Mr. Jonas Yoder was told that the First Amendment protected him and he was not required to send his children to the state school. This case laid down the test that was to be used for all subsequent cases to determine which beliefs are to be protected by the First Amendment and which are not.

The first definition the court made was, "Every religious belief is one of two types. It is either a conviction or a preference."

Most Christians carelessly use the word conviction. In reality, the test of whether or not a matter is a conviction is a very severe one and not to be taken lightly. It will be seen here that most of us possess only preferences.

WHAT IS A PREFERENCE?
A preference is a belief that is held with such intensity that a person can go into full time service in the name of that belief. He can be a minister of the gospel, a Christian schoolteacher or a missionary. He might even give all of his wealth to it and the court decides he still has only a preference. His belief may energize him to stand on a street corner and witness and proselytize, but it would still only be a preference. If a belief can change under some circumstances, the court calls it a preference. True conviction cannot be changed!

1. Peer Pressure
The court has found that peer pressure causes many people to change their beliefs. A minister may study the word of

God and believe that there is something he knows he must do. He resolves in his heart to make that change, but when he shares it with his friends or other ministers or his congregation, they convince him to tone it down a bit so others can cooperate with him. Little by little he bends, proving that what he first said was a preference. He preferred it, he wanted to do it and even resolved to do it, but he changed. The court says that if you can change the belief, it is a preference.

Bear in mind that if a person can ever show from the word of God where something they do is wrong then they must change it. In the context of this topic it refers to peer pressure causing good men to change. In that case the belief is a preference.

2. *People Pressure*

People pressure causes many people to change their beliefs. When a man knows what he believes is right and allows the pressure of others to cause him to bend, the court calls the belief a preference. The court is well aware that the family is probably the strongest influence of change in a person's life. The court says if "family pressure" will cause you to change, your beliefs are preferences.

3. *Lawsuit Pressure*

Lawsuit pressure causes many people to change their beliefs. There have been many men who say, "I am for this, but I am not going to get sued over it because the news media makes us into villains." Defending a ministry against a lawsuit can be very expensive. There are some great victories that are publicized but not many are interested in those who have churches of about 100 that are reduced to 20, or a man with a church of 350 to 400 reduced to 60. If you avoid taking a stand that will cause you to get sued because you do not want to see your church membership drop and that causes you to change your beliefs, then your belief was a preference.

4. *Jail Pressure*

Jail pressure causes many people to change their beliefs. Jails today are thought by some to be like holiday inns but they are horrible places. The incarcerated are isolated from their Christian influence, friends and family. They are told when to go to bed, when to get up, when to eat, how to eat, when to stand, when to sit, when to go to the restroom. And they are thrown into the middle of often-brutal men who normally relish the thought of breaking a Bible-toter.

Would you go to jail for a matter of your faith? Throughout history great men of faith have gone to jail and nobody understood why they went. The court says if you change your beliefs for fear of going to jail, then your beliefs are preferences.

You may believe you could go to jail but would you, as a man, watch your wife go to jail? Levi Whisner, in Ohio, faced that threat and made plans for who was going to take care of their children while he and his wife were incarcerated.

5. *Death Pressure*

Death pressure causes most people to change their beliefs. The court will ask if you are prepared to die for your belief. The court says that for a belief to be a conviction it will not change, even in the face of death. Why? What creates a conviction? For a Christian it is only one thing. He believes that his God requires it of him.

Only a belief that is God-ordered is a conviction. Therefore, the court must first decide if your belief is a conviction or a preference. Only a conviction is protected by the Constitution.

WHAT IS A CONVICTION?

1. *A conviction is something that you purpose in your heart, as a fabric of your belief system.*

It is one that you will not change due to any circumstance. It says, "When you believe that your God has required something of you, you will withstand all of the tests put to you." It has been said that a man is never made by a crisis. The crisis exposes the man for what he already is.

There are parallels to this in the history of the three Hebrew children in the book of Daniel. When taken into captivity, Shadrach, Meshach and Abednego purposed in their hearts not to defile themselves. It was something about which they determined with resolve.

2. *A conviction must be pre-determined.*

When Nebuchadnezzar erected his golden image and commanded that all the people bow when the instruments played, these three men stood erect. A question might be asked at this point, where were all the other Hebrews? There were more than three Hebrews in Babylon who must have been in compliance with the King's orders, for only these three Hebrews, who had predetermined what they would do, remained standing.

3. *A conviction is a personal belief.*

The court says that if you require others to stand with you to maintain your beliefs, then your beliefs are preferences and not convictions. There have been preachers willing to stand on their belief only if they have the backing of a certain college or group to stand with them. That doesn't go over in a court, for your belief must be a personal conviction regardless of what anyone else thinks or does. Shadrach, Meshach, and Abednego did stand together, but in reality they stood alone. Their decision was made more difficult when going against other Hebrews who buckled under the pressure of impending death.

4. *A conviction is non-negotiable.*
When they were brought before the king, Nebuchadnezzar did a strange thing. He broke the law by giving them a second chance. They said to the king that they did not have to be careful how they answered him. They had resolved that they were not going to bow and that was not going to change. They told the king that this was a matter of faith and non-negotiable.

The court says if you can discuss the negotiation of your faith, it is a matter of preference. Why? How do you negotiate what is God ordered? Recall what the three Hebrews said because it illustrates the last point the court chose. "King, we believe that our God can deliver us, but even if you throw us into that furnace and God does not deliver us, we are not going to bow" (Daniel 3:16–18).

5. *A conviction is not contingent on victory.*
The court said if you must be assured of victory before you stand, your beliefs are preferences and not convictions. That is a test the court is beginning to follow because many are more concerned about winning than about standing. Bear this in mind. In the Christian faith we do not fight for victory; we fight in victory. The battle was won at the cross of Calvary and we stand in that victory.

When Levi Whisner went to trial and lost, he still won. When he appealed and lost, he won. When he went to the Supreme Court of the state of Ohio and the judges unanimously said he was right, he was right all along. A court does not tell us whether we are right or wrong. We are right as long as we honor the word of God. Levi recognized that. He stood in this country when no other man saw the issue. He stood for all of us. He stood with no one beside him. When all the tests of preference and conviction were applied, he passed.

THE ULTIMATE TEST OF CONVICTION

The court recognizes a problem because people sometimes do not tell the truth. In the courtroom I have seen some men who have been incredibly casual with the truth. The court decided there must be a way to know whether what is being claimed is the truth, if it is preference or conviction. Real convictions will have already passed the other preference tests: peer pressure, people pressure, lawsuit pressure, jail pressure and death pressure.

6. *A conviction will be demonstrated by a person's lifestyle.*

The court said you do not have the right to say you have a conviction unless it can be seen that the conviction is lived with some degree of consistency. When the court begins to apply that test, good Christian people often become quite uncomfortable.

The word of God says in James that faith is dead without corresponding works. It is like a body with no spirit and is meaningless, because the thing that gives it vibrancy and life is absent. The court will examine the evidence of your faith in action in order to prove it is a conviction.

For example, it may be claimed that children ought to be sent to a Bible based Christian school, believing it to be the only desirable place for them to receive an education that will equip them for life. However, if you do not send your child to a Christian school, then have your child be the best witness he can be in the public school. The court said that is a classic example of a preference statement.

The court is looking for consistency. If we say that something is a matter of conviction, the source of those beliefs is the word of God. We teach a child that it is a sin to disobey the word of God. The court says the opposite of conviction must be a sin and you must act on that belief or else it is not a conviction.

We really cannot take exception to being required to be consistent because that is in line with our beliefs. If the Bible requires it, it is God ordered. If it is God ordered and we choose not to do it, it is a sin. A Christian believes that disobedience to what God has ordered is the classic definition of sin.

According to the court, stating that something is a conviction, you must be prepared to say that its opposite is a sin. If you say you have a conviction about Christian education, then you must be prepared to say that to not give a child a Christian education is a sin. If you say that you have a conviction about a certain lifestyle, then you must say the opposite is a sin, or it is not a conviction. When a person says he ought to do some things, but wants to be more tolerant and a little more open minded, the court determines it a preference.

In the courtroom you must be able to define what you believe. You must tell the court whether you hold your beliefs as preferences or convictions and be able to explain to the court that the opposite of these convictions is a sin. What happens if you don't tell them it is a sin? The following is dialogue that I have personally witnessed:

7.   *A conviction is consistent to itself.*

In this matter of lifestyle consistency, the court says that consistent practice means reasonably consistent, not perfect. One judge said to me, "Your people do not have to be perfect, but they are becoming very perfect at being imperfect. I would like you to see if we could match up the two L's—Life and Lip." A good part of every court case is about whether what you say with your mouth is consistently being practiced with your life. Let us examine how easily we form convictions that can be challenged in court.

It is a conviction of Christians that pornography should not be viewed, that obscenity should not be spoken, that nudity should not be viewed. It is a conviction that unrighteous themes should not be exalted. Most would agree that these are the convictions of a Christian because the Bible requires it. Is it a sin to do otherwise? Yes. These are things that most of us believe.

Your life is the truest test of your convictions. Many Christians live lives that defy their stated beliefs, being against sin in some forms that they readily accept in another form. They denounce the actions of some that they allow to be acceptable in themselves.

The problem we face here is that convictions are being tested and for most of us that scrutiny will verify that many of our so-called convictions are merely preferences. Most of us claim that we would die for beliefs that we are not even consistently living for in other areas of our lives. We have convictions for morality in the school that we do not enforce in our own living rooms. This proves that most of our beliefs are only preferences that we personally find comfortable and convenient.

The greatest tragedy is not the inconsistency before the court, but the insult before Christ. Far too often we bow before the altar of self-serving living and bring a reproach upon the Savior who bought us with the price of His own blood. It is a sad commentary on our love and commitment to Him that we have very few beliefs that could stand up to the serious examination of this world. The greatness of the New Testament church was that the believers were not only willing to die for their beliefs, but their accusers could find no fault or inconsistency in them. Oh, that the world could say the same about us. Someone has said, "Your walk talks and your talk talks, but your walk talks louder than your talk talks."

Perhaps it is time to place ourselves on trial to see if we really believe what we say we believe. Are we really living consistently by the things that we say are convictions? Whether or not you are ever brought to a courtroom and put on trial by men, you are on trial every day before your God. He demands holy living and consistency of life, not just in simplicity of word. Anyone can say he believes in certain things, but as a child of God we ought to live like it. God help us to make it so.

Chapter Three: The Gospels

When God created Adam then took a rib from him to make Eve, He gave them authority over His tremendous creation (Genesis 1:26-28). In verse 28, He told them to do five things: be fruitful, multiply, fill the earth, subdue it, and have dominion over it. The word 'subdue' indicates there would be something that would rise up against them, so does the phrase "have dominion over." In Genesis three we find out what that opponent was, "the serpent."

When they disobeyed God and took of the fruit of the tree of the knowledge of good and evil, they died spiritually and had their relationship with God broken. Because of that, sin entered the human race. Satan began his attempts to gain control over the whole world. The Apostle Paul in 2 Corinthians 4:4 called him, "…the god of this age…" He has been blinding the minds of people ever since the Garden.

We can trace good and evil all the way through the Old Testament as the nation of Israel faced challenge after challenge from enemy nations who attempted to destroy them and often did bring them into captivity when Israel disobeyed God. But when Israel would repent God would deliver them and use them mightily.

The Apostle Paul says in 1 Corinthians 10:11, "Now all these things happened to them as examples and they were written for our admonition, upon whom the ends of the ages have come."

Jesus said in Luke 16:16, "The law and the prophets were until John, since that time the kingdom of God has been preached, and everyone is pressed into it." The preaching of the kingdom of God indicates some important changes.[9]

The kingdom of God message does not negate spiritual warfare, but in some cases amplifies it, and after the Cross assures us of victory because of what Jesus did for us there.

Jesus' earthly ministry consisted of four things, preaching the gospel of the kingdom, teaching, healing, and delivering the demonized. He knew what was in the heart of humanity (John 2:24-25). He knew the depth of their depravity and the changes there were needed to change their heart. He knew the opposition they would face from Satan and his kingdom. He knew that He would need to demonstrate for them, and us, how to live victoriously and minister that victory to those that have not received it.

A cursory reading of the Gospels reveals that dealing with people in general and governments in particular allows us to see spiritual warfare and a need, on occasion, to do civil disobedience.

At the time of Jesus' ministry Rome ruled over the land. Their beliefs and ideology was contrary to the kingdom of God. A good example of that is Jesus' birth and how Joseph and Mary dealt with it (Matthew 2).

Jesus prepared His disciples to face opposition to the kingdom message in His Sermon on the Mount. Matthew 5 10-12 says, "Blessed are those who are persecuted for

---

[9] I suggest reading the book of Hebrews specifically chapters 7-10 to get a better idea of this.

righteousness sake, for theirs is the kingdom of heaven. Blessed are you when they revile and persecute you, and say all kinds of evil against you falsely for my sake. Rejoice and be exceedingly glad, for great is your reward in heaven, for so they persecuted the prophets who were before you." Here we find Jesus telling them that evil will come but rather than revolt against it to realize that it is working for their ultimate benefit! Persecution for righteousness sake is refining and rewarding, what a thought![10]

Jesus went further in Matthew 5:38-42 when He said, "You have heard that it was said, 'an eye for an eye and a tooth for a tooth.' But I tell you not to resist an evil person. But whoever slaps you on your right cheek, turn the other to him also. If anyone wants to sue you and take away your tunic, let him have your cloak also. And who ever compels you to go one mile, go with him two. Give to him who asks you, and from him who wants to borrow from you do not turn away." It seems He is telling them, and us, to respond to those who would mistreat us in the opposite spirit by doing good to them.

He further amplifies this in Matthew 5:44-45, "But I say to you, love your enemies, bless those who curse you, do good to those who hate you, and pray for those who spitefully use you and persecute you, that you may be sons of your Father in heaven, for He makes His sun rise on the evil and on the good, and sends rain on the just and on the unjust."

Notice the things He tells us to do: Love, Bless, Do Good, and Pray for those who spitefully use and persecute you! If we respond this way, we are acting like sons and daughters of our Father!

Jesus tells them, and us, that persecutions are coming. In Matthew 10:16-19, "Behold, I send you out as sheep in

---

[10] 1 Peter 3:13-17, 1 Peter 4:14-17

the midst of wolves. Therefore, be wise as serpents and harmless as doves. But beware of men, for they will deliver you up to councils and scourge you in their synagogues. You will be brought before governors and kings for my sake, as a testimony to them and to the Gentiles. But when they deliver you up, do not worry about how or what you should speak, for it will be given to you in that hour what you should speak."

A lesson I get from these statements is *that we are not ready to stand against earthly authorities until we have done the things Jesus mentions here!*

Chapter Four: APR

HOW THE DISCIPLES RESPONDED

On the Day of Pentecost Peter called his generation "evil or crooked" (Acts 2:40). This gives an idea what to expect in the upcoming accounts about to be given to us. After the healing of the lame man in Acts 3 and the disciples preaching in Solomon's Portico, the religious leaders were greatly disturbed (Acts 4:1-3). They brought the disciples before them and demanded to know by what power or name had they done these things. Peter responds on behalf of the rest and declared boldly that it was through Jesus that the healing and other miracles had been done. After removing the disciples, the council discussed what was to be done to them. The council demanded that they no longer speak or teach in the name of Jesus, to which Peter and John declared, "Whether it is right in the sight of God to listen to you more than to God, you judge. For we cannot but speak the things which we have seen and heard' (Acts 5:18-19). After being threatened and let go, they went back to the others and had a great prayer meeting. Part of their prayer was for themselves for God to "...grant to your servants that with all boldness they may speak your word, by stretching out your hand to heal, and that signs and wonders may be done through the name of your holy servant Jesus (Acts 4:29-30) The result? "And when they had prayed, the place where they were assembled together was shaken, and they were all filled with the Holy Spirit, and they spoke the word of God with boldness." (Acts 4:31)

Acts 5 reveals the divine discipline of the Lord on Ananias and Sapphira who lied to God and both of them died. Afterward through the hands of the apostles many signs and miracles were done and the believers were more dedicated than before (Acts 5:12-16). This infuriated the high priest and the Sadducees, who had the apostles thrown into prison but an angel from God got them out which resulted in them being put on trial again. When reminded that the council had told them not to speak about Jesus, Peter and the other apostles responded, "We ought to obey God rather than man." (Acts 5:29)

So what did the apostles & disciples do when persecuted?

- They remained faithful to the Lord and His Word.
- They prayed fervently.
- They spoke boldly.
- They continued to obey God rather than man.

The lesson we learn from this is *that it is always better to obey God when earthly governments persecute us.*

Saul was persecuting the church and giving testimony against the disciples. However, he met the Lord on the Damascus Road and was healed, filled with the Holy Spirit, and became a mighty apostle. Because of his bold preaching, and miracles that occurred in his ministry, he faced persecution consistently. Reading the last half of the book of Acts reveals all that he suffered. This was something God had told Ananias when He sent him to minister to Saul (Acts 9:15-16). Saul's life was so dramatically different that God changed his name from Saul to Paul.

Appeal

After united prayer for those who persecute us, sometimes it is right to appeal to higher authorities (Acts 25:12). Paul had been left in prison for two years by Festus who did nothing to resolve the threats made against Paul by Roman guards. After making his appeal, Paul was given several opportunities to give his testimony and to share the good news to many of the authorities both Jewish and Roman.

This is in keeping with the First Amendment to the U.S. Constitution, which says, "Congress shall make no law respecting an establishment of religion, or prohibiting the free exercise thereof; or abridging the freedom of speech, or of the press; or the right of the people peaceably to assemble, and to petition the Government for a redress of grievances."

So we have a constitutional right to appeal grievances by appealing to a higher authority. The highest human government authority in the USA is the Supreme Court.

Protest

In 2019 in Kentucky as well as several other states, many of the school teachers gathered in their state capitol to protest the lack of funding for teacher salaries and supplies. As long as it is 'peaceable' it is permitted.

In Acts 23 while Paul was testifying before the council, he saw that it was divided between Sadducees and Pharisees and began to proclaim that he was a Pharisee. This pleased the Pharisees on the council but a protest broke out then between the two groups. Because of Paul's commitment to Jesus' Lordship he often found himself in such circumstances. In the near future this may be our lot as well.

Revolt

On December 16, 1773 the colonists revolted against England over 'taxation without representation.' This became an important event in the establishment of the laws of our country.

In 1989 there was a large protest/revolt in Tiananmen Square, China that was set off by the death of pro-reform Communist general secretary Hu Yaobang in April 1989, amid the backdrop of rapid economic development and social changes in post-Mao China, the protests reflected anxieties about the country's future in the popular consciousness and among the political elite. The protests of 1989 were organized by groups of students, intellectuals and labor activists. There was no common cause or leadership in the protests. However, most protesters did not like the way the Communist party of China ran the economy. Some people also wanted a change towards more democracy. A massacre occurred when 300,000 soldiers arrived. And over two days they killed over 2000 people and 7000 more were wounded. As terrible as these deaths were, they pale in comparison to what happens in our country each year when at least 750,000 pre-born babies are killed in the abortion clinics!

Obedience verse Submission

This has been an area of much misunderstanding and abuse through the centuries. There is a place for doing what the New Testament instructs us to do with each of these great truths.

Let's look at a few passages to see what the Scriptures say.

Submit

- 1 Corinthians 16:15-16 "…household of Stephanas…have devoted themselves to the ministry of the saints –that you also submit to such, and to everyone who works and labors with us."
- Ephesians 5:21 "Submitting to one another in the fear (reverence) of God."

- Ephesians 5:22 "Wives, submit to your own husbands, as to the Lord."
- 1 Peter 2:13 "Therefore submit yourselves to every ordinance of man for the Lord's sake, whether to the king as supreme…:
- 1 Peter 5:5 "Likewise, you younger people, submit yourselves to your elders, yes, all of you be submissive to one another, and be clothed with humility."

Obedience
- Acts 5:19 "We ought to obey God rather than men."
- Ephesians 6:1 "Children, obey your parents in the Lord, for this is right."
- Colossians 3:21 "Bondservants, obey in all things your masters according to the flesh, not with eyeservice, as menpleasers, but in sincerity of heart, fearing God."
- Hebrews 13:17 "Obey those who rule over you and be submissive, for they watch out for your souls, as those who must give account. Let them do so with joy and not with grief, for that would be unprofitable for you."
- Titus 3:1 "Remind them to be subject to rulers and authorities, to obey, to be ready for every good work."

Do these statements apply to governing authorities? Only in the church? Obviously, they do apply to family order. How far can this be taken without becoming slavery? We will deal with these questions in the next chapter when we get to Romans 13.

Chapter Five:
Romans 13

In 1972 I attended a week long seminar at McCormick Place in Chicago led by Bill Gothard. A statement that he made at that time has stuck with me since. He said "one of the most important things one can do is to learn to recognize and submit to authority. Once he has learned that he can be a success in any environment."

"Let every soul be subject to the governing authorities. For there is no authority except from God, and the authorities that exist are appointed by God. Therefore, whoever resists the authority resists the ordinance of God, and those who resist will bring judgment on themselves. For rulers are not a terror to good works, but to evil. Do you want to be unafraid of the authority? Do what is good, and you will have praise from the same. For he is God's minister to you for good. But if you do evil, be afraid; for he does not bear the sword in vain; for he is God's minister, an avenger to execute wrath on him who practices evil. Therefore, you must be subject, not only because of wrath but also for conscience' sake. For because of this you also pay taxes, for they are God's ministers attending continually to this very thing. Render therefore to all their due: taxes to whom taxes are due, customs to whom customs, fear to whom fear, honor to whom honor. Owe no one anything except to love one another, for he who loves another has fulfilled the law." Romans 13:1-8

This passage has been the basis for much discussion, especially in times of persecution and government overreach. There are those who read this passage and declare, without any qualifications, that any person in any authoritative position has been put there by God and must explicitly be obeyed. And if this passage is seen just by itself without any other considerations then it is easy to see why they would believe this way.

God is the source of all legitimate authority!

The second sentence of verse one says "For there is no authority except from God, and the authorities that exist are appointed by God." This is in agreement with what Jesus said in Matthew 28:18, "And Jesus came and spoke to them, saying, All authority has been given to me in heaven and on earth."[11] If authority exists anywhere in the universe its source is from God. However, not everyone who claims authority or is in a position over other people has been put there by God. The context of our study is within the revelation of the New Covenant. Can we honestly say that Hitler was ordained by God to kill six million Jews?

But in the process of answering that question we must consider that because someone in a position of authority does evil does not mean that they were not originally placed there by God. Consider Cyrus who was called by God "My shepherd" and "my Anointed One." [12] He was extremely wicked yet God used him for a specific task for Israel.

---

[11] Daniel 7:13-14

[12] Isaiah 44:28 Isaiah 45:1

Some people see Romans 13 as applying more to authorities in the church than secular authorities in governments. It certainly is applicable to church government, but I would not limit it to just that.

So it comes down to how we relate to those who are in a position of authority. We gave several passages of Scripture in chapter four about submission and obedience. We should know that one major difference is *that submission speaks of an attitude and obedience speaks of an outward action.* One can be made to obey but still have an attitude of rebellion within. Or one may have an attitude of submission but lovingly not obey what the authority is demanding.

We see examples in Acts of the early church defying when the Roman and Jewish authorities demanded they cease their preaching about Jesus. They keep doing it and willingly suffered the punishment of doing so.

As we pointed out earlier in chapter one Dietrich Bonhoeffer believed it was a Christian's right and duty to oppose tyranny which is no longer based on natural law and the law of God. Francis Schaeffer believed a Christian is bound to resist the state by whatever means necessary-through direct legal and political action and possible demonstrations of civil disobedience. He believed that when the state defies the absolute law of God, its authority becomes illegitimate.

How do we determine when it is right to resist authority? What criteria do we use to do so? Is it philosophic differences? Moral issues such as abortion? Mistreatment of minorities? Demanding certain actions such as quarantine in your homes during a pandemic? Racial issues? Political parties? Cultural differences? Religious beliefs?

I submit to you that while one or more of these might be involved, I believe it comes down to authority that *demands we obey them when we would have to disobey*

God to do so. If we are told we cannot read the Bible, pray, or worship God then it is the time to resist. If authority demands that we worship another god other than Jehovah or Jesus, then we resist. If authority demands that we close our church, then we resist even though we know the church is more than a building and in other countries when this has happened (China) the church continued to thrive.

St Augustine is quoting as saying, "an unjust law is no law at all." This quote was also repeated by Dr. Martin Luther King, Jr. [13]

There are different interpretations and applications of the laws of the land. Who are we to believe? The recent pandemic of the coronavirus is a good example of that! One set of health experts says a certain thing is the best while another group of medical experts says the opposite.

One group of people believes that we must obey to the nth degree what the health experts say or we are not loving our neighbor. Another group thinks that we should choose the ones that best suit our individual family or congregation.

---

[13] "One may well ask: 'How can you advocate breaking some laws and obeying others?' The answer lies in the fact that there are two types of laws: just and unjust. I would be the first to advocate obeying just laws. One has not only a legal but a moral responsibility to obey just laws. Conversely, one has a moral responsibility to disobey unjust laws. I would agree with St. Augustine that 'an unjust law is no law at all.'

"Now, what is the difference between the two? How does one determine whether a law is just or unjust? A just law is a man-made code that squares with the moral law or the law of God. An unjust law is a code that is out of harmony with the moral law. To put it in the terms of St. Thomas Aquinas: An unjust law is a human law that is not rooted in eternal law and natural law. Any law that uplifts human personality is just. Any law that degrades human personality is unjust." *Letter from Birmingham Jail*

I believe if or when circumstances get to the point we have to decide to resist authority, we need to examine our life to see if our decision is based on preferences or convictions. Another thing to consider is, where is the Holy Spirit leading us and what is He saying about this situation. Our decision should not be based on a whim or a spur of the moment emotion. Perhaps we should ask ourselves what would Jesus do? Or what does the love of God compel us to do?

I also believe such decisions should not be made alone but in the context of family and the local church where we are planted. We should follow the leading of the Holy Spirit and give less weight to the secular media!

Chapter Six: What About Love?[14]

In the Greek language, there are four words for love. They are: *agapao, phileo, storgos, eros. Agapao* is the God-type of love which is self-sacrificing. *Phileo* is

---

[14] You have heard that it was said, 'You shall love your neighbor and hate your enemy.' But, I say to you, love your enemies, bless those who curse you, do good to those who hate you, and pray for those who spitefully use you and persecute you. Matthew 5:43-44

Jesus said to him, "'You shall love the LORD your God with all your heart, with all your soul, and with all your mind.' Matthew 22:37

And the second is like it: 'You shall love your neighbor as yourself.' Matthew 22:39

A new commandment I give to you, that you love one another; as I have loved you, that you also love one another. John 13:34

Greater love has no one than this, than to lay down one's life for his friends. John 15:13

Now hope does not disappoint, because the love of God has been poured out in our hearts by the Holy Spirit who was given to us. Romans 5:5

Love does no harm to a neighbor; therefore, love is the fulfillment of the law. 1 Corinthians 13:10

brotherly love. *Storgos* is a parental love for one's child. Eros is sexual love. In this chapter we will put emphasis on the first two.

"Though I speak with the tongues of men and of angels, but have not love, I have become sounding brass or a clanging cymbal. And though I have the gift of prophecy, and understand all mysteries and all knowledge, and though I have all faith, so that I could remove mountains, but have not love, I am nothing. And though I bestow all my goods to feed the poor, and though I give my body to be burned, but have not love, it profits me nothing. Love suffers long and is kind; love does not envy; love does not parade itself, is not puffed up; does not behave rudely, does not seek its own, is not provoked, thinks no evil; does not rejoice in iniquity, but rejoices in the truth; bears all things, believes all things, hopes all things, endures all things. Love never fails. But whether there are prophecies, they will fail; whether there are tongues, they will cease; whether there is knowledge, it will vanish away." 1 Corinthians 13:1-8

In this passage every place the word *love* is used, it is the Greek word *agapao* which is the God-type of love. The one characteristic that defines God to us is His love! God is patient and kind, He is longsuffering, etc. But all these attributes come from His love. [15]

Okay, so how does this relate to civil disobedience?

We can approach any situation with love or with ruthlessness, arrogance, and hate. As a Christian we are admonished to live our lives out of the God-kind of love. The outcomes of our response will be aligned with the hate/love that we approach the situation.

On numerous occasions I have prayed, along with others, in front of the abortion clinic on the corner of Market and Second Street in downtown Louisville. Some

---

[15] 1 John 4:7-10

of the picketers have shown anger, shouting at, and saying derogatory remarks to the escorts from the clinic. This produces no positive results. On the other hand, on several occasions I have seen the women going in to the clinic change their mind and receive counsel and prayer from those who acted out of kindness and love. 1 Corinthians 13:8 says, "Love never fails." Why? If we act from *agapao* type love it is God Himself (God is love) flowing out of us into the person or situation.

When we are considering an appeal, protest, revolt or some other type of action that could lead to civil disobedience, we need to be sure that our heart motivation is done out of God's love from within.

Checklist

- o Is it a Preference or Conviction?
- o Are you recognizing the authority and do you have a submitted attitude toward it?
- o Is what the authority is demanding you do contrary to plain statements of Scripture?
- o Are you expressing the love of God for those in authority?
- o Have you spent time in prayer for those in authority to the point that your conscience is clear as it relates to them?

Doing acts of civil disobedience is not to be taken lightly. It is easy when persecuted to get in the flesh and lash out at those who are doing us wrong. We should respond to them in the opposite spirit. My thought is that civil disobedience should be the last thing one does after having exhausted all other avenues.

May God help us to know His voice and leading in such matters!

Other Books By Dr. Carroll Parish

BECOMING WHO YOU ARE - $3.00

This book shows who we are in Christ and who He wants to be in us. There are 168 things that He has provided for us through the Cross. They are all referenced in this little book.

TURNING THE CURSE INTO BLESSING - $3.00

Curses operate in everyone's life to some degree. In this book we discover how we can turn the curse around and be blessed instead.

THE MOST OFTEN GIVEN COMMAND - $3.00

Of all the commands in the Scriptures, there is one that is given more often than the others. This book is about how you and I can obey this command every day in every circumstance.

SICK AND TIRED - $3.00

This book is about what you can do to regain your health by using natural means, or stay healthy by diet and lifestyle.

LIVING OUT OF YOUR SPIRIT - $3.00

This book shows us how to live out of our spirit instead of the body or the mind. Everyone should read it.

SPIRITUAL WARFARE – ENGAGING THE ENEMY - $3.00

This book gives the principles of how to engage the devil and win! It is based on over 50 years of experience in Bible study and the deliverance ministry.

CURRENT EVENTS IN LIGHT OF THE END-TIMES - $3.00

This book looks at Scripture to find meaning for the situations of our day. If one is concerned about what is seen today, this book is a must read.

MORE PRECIOUS THAN RUBIES - $3.00

This book looks at the value and availability of wisdom from the first nine chapters of Proverbs and other passages. It is combined with AMAZING GRACE into one cover. A two for one special.

AMAZING GRACE - $3.00

This book looks at the two manifestations of the grace of God. His grace is revealed as unmerited favor and Divine ability. It also shows us how to not offend the grace of God.

APPOINTED TO DEATH – RAISED TO LIFE - $3.00

This book shares about death from a positive perspective of the Word of God. Everyone should read it to be better prepared for what awaits us all.

OUR GREAT SALVATION - $3.00

This book is about the wonderful things that have been provided for us through the sacrifice of Jesus on the Cross.

Read it and discover that there may have been more there than you have seen before.

HEALING MINISTRY OF JESUS - $3.00
This book covers the four-fold ministry of Jesus with emphasis on His healings. It shows how His early disciples continued it and that it continues even into today. A very helpful book on healing.

HOLY SPIRIT AND HIS GIFTS - $3.00
This book teaches about the ministry of the Holy Spirit in the church today and how we can cooperate with Him to do the will of God.

ANGELS WATCHING OVER ME - $3.00
This little book covers some basic things about the ministry of angels. There have been many accounts of angel encounters in recent time. This will help us get a Biblical understanding of their work in our day.

PROPHETS ON ASSIGNMENT - $3.00
This book helps us understand the ministry of prophets from both the Old Testament and New Testament. It helps us comprehend the gift of prophecy and its place in the Church today.

OVERCOMING THE TRIUMVIRATE OF EVIL - $ 3.00
In this book we put emphasis on overcoming the flesh, the devil and the world. We emphasize the point that the victory has been provided for us but it is necessary for each believer in Jesus to appropriate it for himself.

A FUNNY THING HAPPENED ON THE WAY TO THE PULPIT - $ 3.00
This book covers humorous events and life lessons learned

over the last 50 years of ministry. You will see how the hand of God took care of some very dangerous situations and at other times very hilarious situations.

THE MIRACLE WORKER - $ 3.00

This book gives an overview of miracles from both the Old & New Testament. It is faith building and encourages us to believe God for miracles in our daily lives.

THE WONDER OF WORSHIP - $ 3.00

This book gives an overview of the importance and power of worship. A must read for every believer!

HOW TO FACE DEATH LIKE A CHRISTIAN - $ 3.00

This little book helps us to see how a Christian can and should deal with the death of a family member or friend. There are many examples given of those in the Bible who did so.

DISCERNING SPIRITUAL REALITIES - $ 3.00

This book informs us about what is going on around us in the unseen realm. Very encouraging!

THE PROBLEM OF HUMAN SEXUALITY, and what to do about it. - $ 3.00

This book identifies one of the greatest problems in our society today and provides answers and help for those involved with same-sex attractions.

THE GOSPEL OF GRACE - $10.99

This is a layman's commentary on Romans 5-8. It gives a verse by verse explanation of the great truths found there. It is available on Amazon in both hard copy and for Kindle at $6.99.

RICH BEYOND MEASURE - $10.99

This is a layman's commentary on the book of Ephesians. It reveals our great wealth we possess in Jesus. It also reveals how we should walk it out in daily life. It is available on Amazon in both hard copy and for Kindle at $6.99.

IN EVERYTHING GOD WORKS - $3.00

This book is an exegesis of Romans 8:28. It will prove to be very enlightening to those who read it and will encourage us to seek God and His will for our life.

KEYS TO OPENING THE WINDOWS OF HEAVEN - $3.00

This book covers how generosity brings the blessings of God. We should learn to be generous with our time, talents, truth & tithe. We will learn how to give beyond the tithe and see the blessings of God revealed in our life.

THE SHEPHERD AND HIS SHEEP - $4.00

This shows what a real shepherd is like. Jesus sets before us the perfect example of shepherding. Every pastor needs to read and apply what is said herein.

THE KING AND HIS KINGDOM - $8.00

This book shows us some things about the Kingdom of God that has often been overlooked. It gives Scriptural teaching as well as practical applications of doing Kingdom work.

COMMENTARY ON THE BOOK OF JAMES - $4.00

This is a verse by verse exposition of the book of James. We cover the Faith vs. Works mentality as well as the other aspects of this book.

About the Author

Dr. Carroll Parish has been in the ministry over 55 years. He has pastored churches, taught seminars, done short-term mission work in 33 countries, and hosted a weekly program seen nationwide on satellite television. Dr. Parish has a heart to help young pastors and believers to mature in the things of God. He and his wife Debbie have been married 50 years. They have two sons and eight grandchildren.

CONTACT INFORMATION:

Dr. Carroll Parish

3402 Goose Creek Road

Louisville, Ky. 40241

(502) 426-3132

carrollp@newlifechurch-lou.org